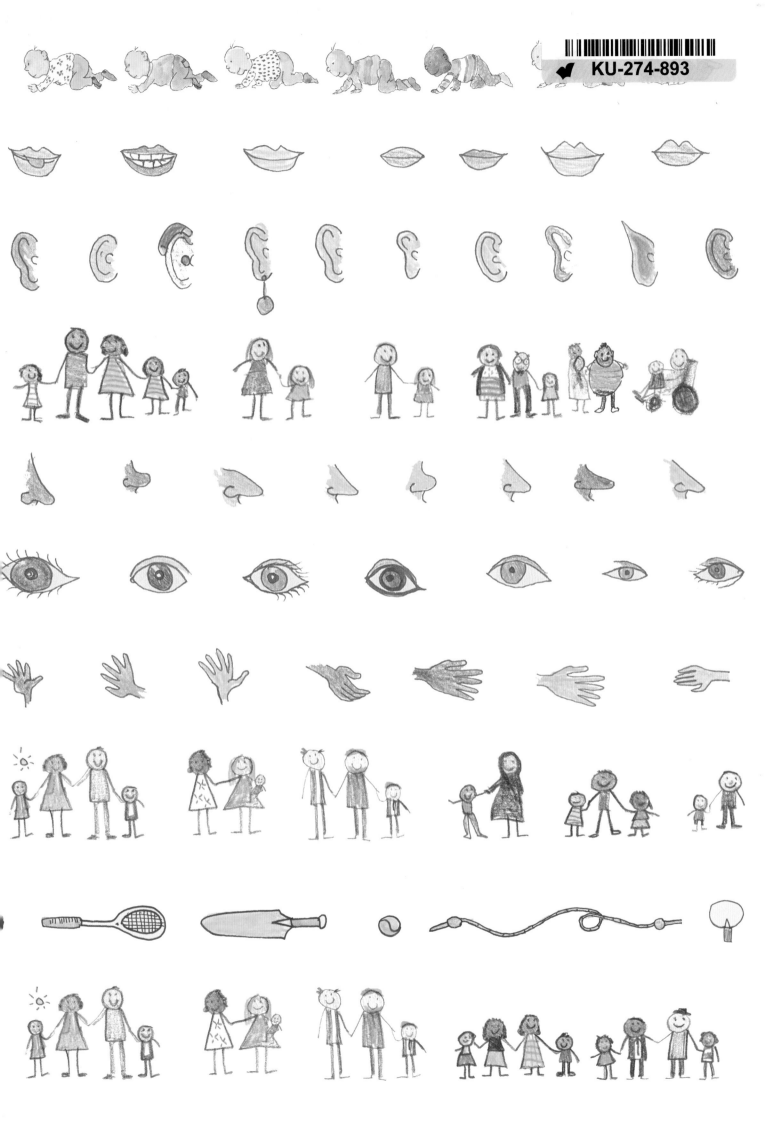

For Juliet and Zeke – M. H.

For Isabel and Josephine – R. A.

With many thanks to Alexandra Strick and Beth Cox of *Inclusive Minds*
for their invaluable assistance and to Dr Jackie Morris MB FRCP
for checking the facts.

JANETTA OTTER-BARRY BOOKS

First published in the UK and the USA in 2016 by Frances Lincoln Children's Books,
an imprint of The Quarto Group,
142 W 36th Street, 4th Floor, New York, NY 10018, U.S.A.
QuartoKnows.com   Visit our blogs at QuartoKids.com

This paperback edition first published in the UK and the USA in 2017

QuartoKnows.com
Visit our blogs at QuartoKids.com

Important: there are age restrictions for most blogging and social media sites and in many countries parental consent is also required.
Always ask permission from your parents. Website information is correct at time of going to press. However, the publishers cannot
accept liability for any information or links found on any Internet sites, including third-party websites.

ISBN 978-1-84780-687-1

Illustrated with watercolours

Printed in China
1 3 5 7 9 8 6 4 2

The Great Big Body Book

Can you find ME every time you turn a page?

Mary Hoffman and Ros Asquith

Frances Lincoln
Children's Books

Everybody Needs

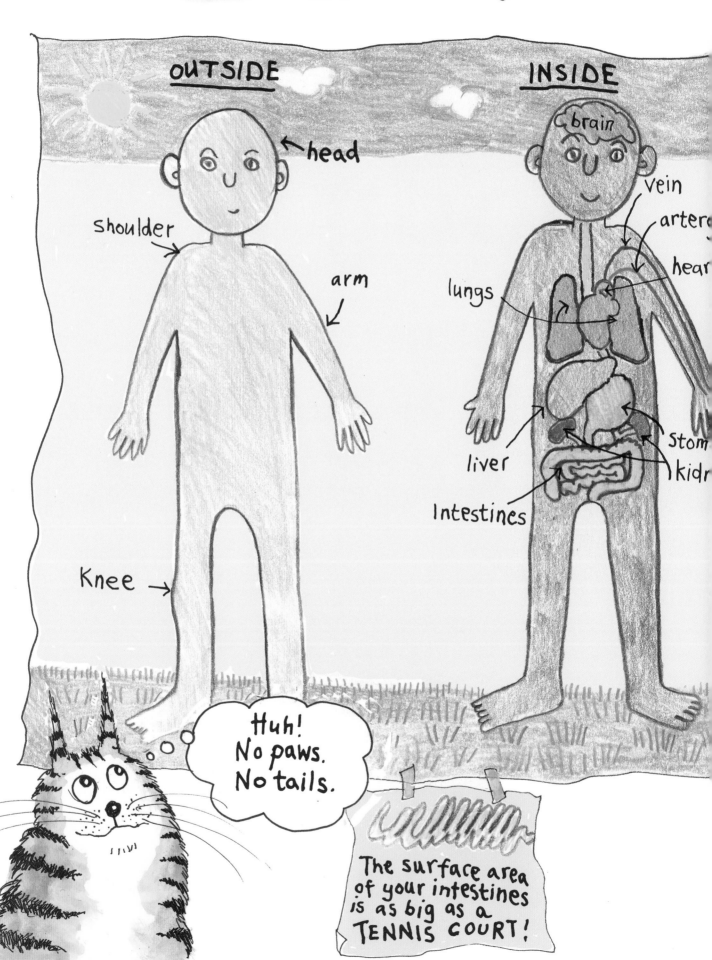

SOME BODY

SKELETON

skull

ibs

spine

elvis

you have over 200 bones!

What is a body? Our bodies are such a large part of us we can't do anything without them.

They aren't the whole story, though. You can't find our thoughts and dreams and wishes anywhere in our bodies.

Why didn't the skeleton go to the DISCO?

He had NO BODY to dance with!

A NEW LIFE

Have you seen a newborn baby lately? They are really small, even the biggest ones. But some are specially tiny, if they get born early. Or if there's more than one of them born together.

New babies have almost everything they will ever need in their bodies, except teeth. And some of them don't have much hair! But most of them know how to suck milk and how to cry to get attention.

doctor

writer

astronaut

Everybody was a baby once. Even the Queen of England!

Some of us were kittens.

police officer

actor

school teacher

dentist

ballet dancer

artist

queen

scientist

And after about six weeks,
babies may even smile!

bus driver

MILESTONES

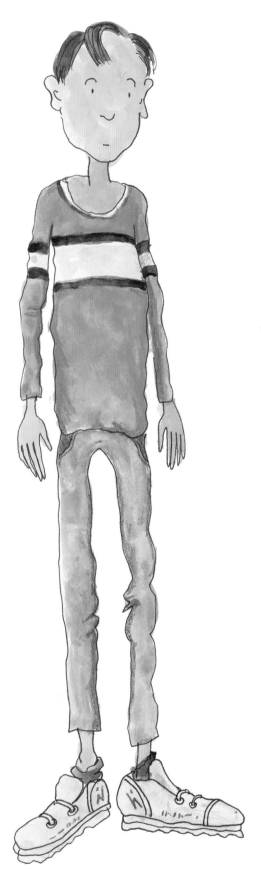

If we kept growing and changing the way that babies do in their first year of life, we'd all be giants!
Babies can go from needing everything done for them and not being able even to support their own heads, to being little people on the verge of walking and talking.

We wanted him to grow up - but not THAT big.

Kittens can walk at FIVE DAYS old...

They grow teeth - and more hair. Their bones get longer, their muscles get stronger and they crawl and toddle about.

Babies start eating more food than just milk – and make a great mess doing it till they learn not to.

Then they stop needing nappies as their bodies tell them when to go to the toilet.

SAME but DIFFERENT

There are TWENTY muscles in your foot.

Your biggest muscle is in your bottom

Bodies come in all shapes and sizes and some different colours. But most of us have the same parts: eyes, ears, noses, arms and hands, legs and feet. And all the important bits inside – our brain, heart, lungs, stomach, liver and kidneys.

But not everyone develops as people expect. Some babies need extra help to get around and talk.

There are so many things that our bodies have to do, it's amazing that most manage to do them all.

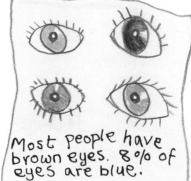

We all have different fingerprints.

Babies have MORE bones than adults.

Just think of all that blood going round inside your body, and your heart pumping away every single day of your life!

You've got 600 muscles, just like me!

And of course there are our bones and muscles that let us move around, run, jump, pick things up, throw things, catch them, carry babies and shopping, play the piano or ride a bike.

Without bones we would just fold up.

Did you know we all have different TONGUE prints?

Our bodies really are wonderful!

Your smallest muscles are in your ears.

We are more alike than different.

Boy or Girl?

The first thing people want to know when
a baby is born is, "Is it a boy or a girl?"

Do you think that pink is a colour for girls
and blue for boys? If so, think again!

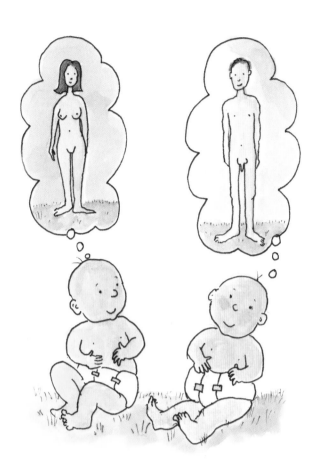

Some bits of your body are different, according to whether you are male or female.

For most people that stays the same throughout life – if you are born a boy you become a man and if a girl, you grow up to be a woman.

But a few don't feel completely comfortable in the body they were born in and not everyone fits neatly into a "boy" or "girl" box. That's OK – just be yourself!

When you are a child, the older you get, the more you can do. You become bigger and stronger and better at doing complicated things. Our bodies, with the help of our brains, can learn some very clever skills.

Everyone's body changes as they grow up. But sometimes there's a big growth spurt and a child can grow several inches taller in one year.

TEENAGERS

Everyone goes through a stage when their bodies change dramatically, at around ten to fourteen years old, though it can be earlier or later.

Don't worry, it's not like breaking a bone.

But I don't WANT my voice to break.

GROWING UP

Boys' voices get deeper and they start growing hair on their faces and private parts. Girls grow breasts and their hips get wider. They get hair in private places too.

All this can feel a bit strange and alarming, but it happens to everyone on the way from being a child to being a grown-up.

Hah! Spots! I prefer stripes.

If you have a teenage brother or sister you may notice they spend ages in front of the mirror. This is a time when we think a lot about what we look like and who we are.

Who am I?

BiG and small

Grown-ups go through body changes too, especially women who have babies. At first you can't see any difference and then, at around four months pregnant, you can see a bump, which gets bigger and bigger until the baby is ready to come out.

Now can we put the baby back inside you?

Baby bumps are not the same as being fat. Imagine how much room it takes up in a woman's body to grow a whole new person!

But some people *are* fat, just as some are thin, some are tall and some are short.

I've got a short arm and a long arm.

And it might not always be because they eat more or less than anyone else. Some very thin people eat a lot and some fat ones eat less. Their different shapes come because of the rate at which their bodies burn up the food they eat.

KEEPING FIT

Food gives our bodies energy and keeps us warm.
It helps us to grow and stay fit and healthy.

You two need fresh air and exercise.

But some foods are better for us than
others. Too much sugar, fat and salt
will make anyone less healthy.

EAT SOME OF THESE EVERY DAY

PROTEIN (nuts, fish, meat, beans)

VEG (carrots, peas, cabbage... lots)

FRUIT (apples, bananas, pears...)

DRINK WATER

RUN about a LOT

Some people work their bodies quite hard at different sports or at the gym. But others don't ask much of their bodies. They are happy to let them lie on the sofa while they watch TV. Or they sit for a long time looking at computer screens or games consoles.

Woolball is cats' football.

That probably *is* expecting too much of their bodies! We all need to move around a bit to keep our bodies working well. Even writers and artists who spend a long time sitting at keyboards and drawing boards!

BREAKS, bruises & being ILL

Nobody stays fit and well all the time. We may fall and break a bone or cut ourselves and need stitches. And even if there are no accidents, we might catch a cold or chickenpox or a tummy bug and feel really ill.

I can't go to school. Teddy's got a cold.

There used to be a lot more childhood illnesses but now babies and children have vaccinations against most of them.

Sometimes you can't just kiss it better.

The body is very good at healing itself – bones mend, bruises fade, skin heals over.

Not every illness can get better but we usually don't feel ill for too long.

I don't get spots but I do get ill.

Ha ha! Spotty!

It's chicken pox.

USiNG our BODIES

Some people can use their bodies to run really fast or play the violin or dance,

or climb mountains or do complicated operations on other people's bodies.

USiNG our MiNDS

But you can't do any of those things without using your brain as well.

And the brain is another part of the body.

Do you think your brain is the same thing as your mind? Doctors can scan a human brain but they can't tell what you are thinking or what you dream at night.

The FIVE SENSES

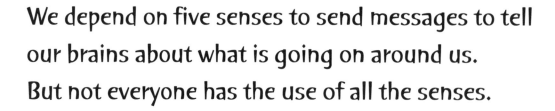

We depend on five senses to send messages to tell our brains about what is going on around us. But not everyone has the use of all the senses.

I use touch to read.

And I use glasses.

Sight – Our eyes can do many things, from judging distances to seeing colour and recognising people and places we know.

Hearing – Sounds travel through our ears and we can tell loud from soft, enjoy music and know our friends' voices, even when we can't see them.

If we can't hear, we can sign!

Cats are supposed to have a sixth sense – but where is it?

Taste – We all have favourite tastes. When you are little you probably love the taste of sweets, but when you are older you may prefer coffee or olives.

Smell – This is very closely linked to taste. If we lose our sense of smell because we have a cold, we can't taste our food so well. We have favourite smells too – fresh bread, hot chocolate, roast potatoes. What are yours?

Can babies smell THEMSELVES?

Touch – Our fingertips are some of the most sensitive parts of our bodies. We can feel the difference between hard and soft, rough and smooth and know what we are touching even if we can't see it.

Five Senses

Sight
Hearing
Taste
Smell
Touch

Please, Miss, where is our sense of humour?

FAMILIES

How we look, and maybe even how well our five senses work, depends partly on our parents and grandparents. Some things, like red hair or being good at balancing, run in families. And so do things like being musical or good at drawing or best at maths and science.

My grandpa is Jamaican, my grandma has red hair, my dad is blind and my mum is an acrobat. And me? I take after ALL of them.

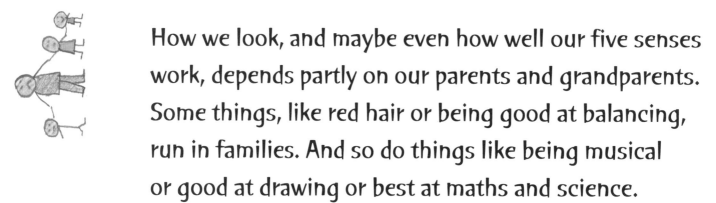

He's got my hair.

And, if there are twins in our family, we are more likely to have twins ourselves.

Imagine if you are one of quadruplets! And if you all had four children at the same time ....

Ha! Only four. I've got SIX.

When we are very old, some of the things that happen when we are small start to happen the other way round. Our hair may get thinner and sometimes disappears altogether. The teeth that we had some trouble growing might fall out.

Teiichi Igarashi climbed Mount Fuji aged 100!

Mary Wesley published her first adult novel aged 71!

Cellist Pablo Casals conducted his own composition aged 94!

Grandma Moses started painting in her 70s!

We might not be so active any more when we are old. But people are living longer now and they can feel fit and well at a hundred years old and more. Most older people are still having a great time and they have a lifetime of memories.

MY LIFE

DEAD BODIES

Still, one day the body will wear out and then
the person dies. And that's another meaning
of the word "body" – the bits that are left over
after death.

Because we love that person, we treat their body
with respect. But that is not who they were, is it?

That is the person who lives on in our
memories of them, their laugh or the way
they made us feel better when we were sad,
or the fantastic apple pies they made.

I miss
Grandpa.

Me too. But we
can still speak
to him in our minds.

Different but SAME

We, the two people who made this book, have bodies that look very different. Ros is tall and thin while Mary is short and round. But we are both women, both have had children, and both used our bodies – and our minds – to bring you this book.

Me? I'm short and FURRY.

We hope you've enjoyed it, and that it has made you think about your amazing body and all the things it can do.

What are YOU like?

 # SOME USEFUL WORDS

Blood – Blood delivers important substances such as nourishment and oxygen to the cells and takes away waste from the same cells. A cell is the basic structure of all living things including humans.

Bones – Every single person has a skeleton made of bones. Bones are hard and give our bodies structure and help us move and stand, as well as protecting our inside organs.

Brain – This is the organ inside our skull which not only sends and delivers messages to and from our muscles and organs but also thinks for us.

Heart –The heart is a very strong muscle which pumps blood all over the body.

Intestines – Also called bowels or guts, these are the muscular tubes leading from the stomach, where food continues to be processed, to where faeces (poo) are pushed out of the body.

Kidneys – A pair of organs that removes waste and produces urine (pee).

Liver – An organ that helps to clean the blood.

Lungs – Two organs in the chest that breathe in oxygen and breathe out carbon dioxide.

Muscles – Bands of tissue that stretch and contract so we can move our limbs.

Organs – Parts of the body that have one particular, very important function, like the heart or kidneys.

Pregnant – A woman who is pregnant is carrying a baby inside her body.

Quadruplets – Four babies who are carried in a woman's body at the same time.

Skin – This is the largest organ in the human body! It's a layer of stretchy tissue that covers the whole body.

Stomach – The stomach is a stretchy bag on the left side of the body, below the chest, which breaks down food before it is sent down to the intestines.

Twins – Two babies who are carried in a woman's body at the same time.

Vaccination – An injection or medicine to prevent common illnesses.

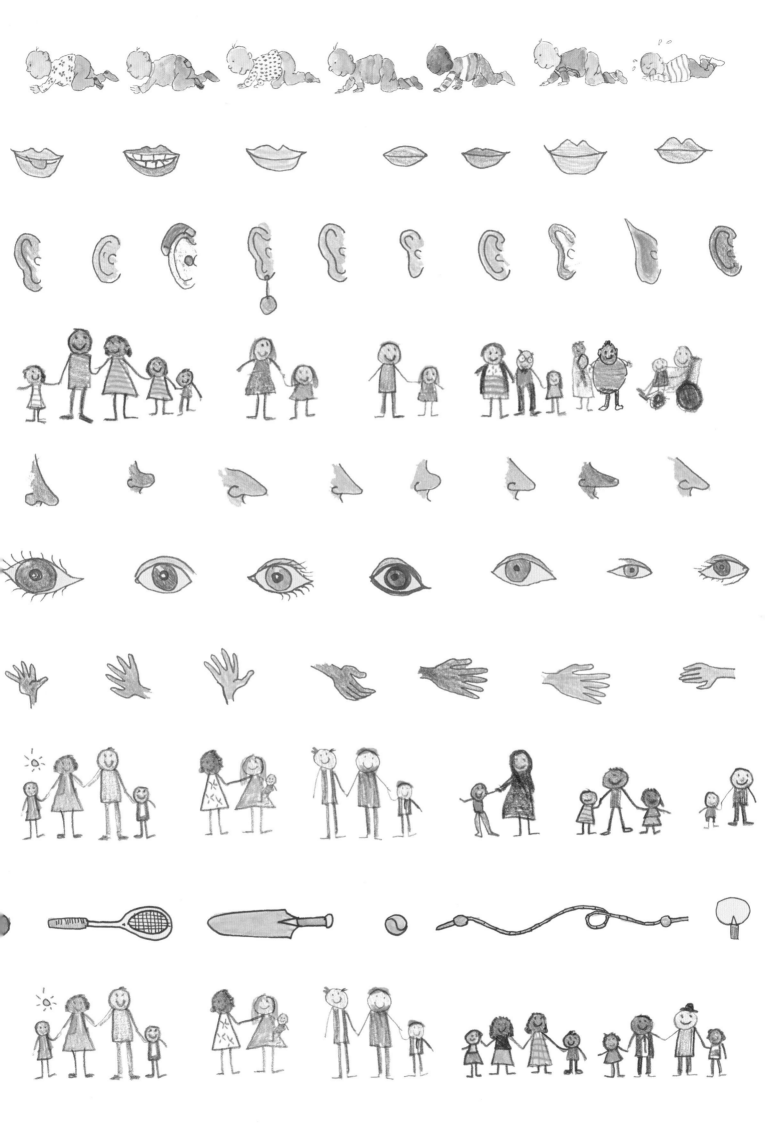

MORE TITLES IN THE FANTASTIC GREAT BIG BOOKS SERIES:

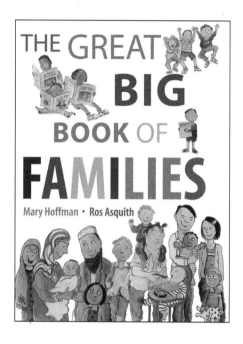

The Great Big Book of Families

Who's in your family?

Some people have lots of brothers and sisters, and uncles and aunties and cousins, and grandmas and grandpas and great-grandmas and great-grandpas...

But some people have really small families.

You can be a family with just two people.

978-1-84780-587-4

Winner of the
SLA Information Book Award

"A superb book" – *Child Care*

"Thoughtful and joyful" – *LoveReading*

"Something for everyone in this truly multicultural exploration" – *School Librarian*

The Great Big Book of Feelings

How do you feel today? Happy? Sad? Jealous? Excited? Silly?

Or a mixture of all the above and more...?

Explore lots of different feelings, see if you can find feelings that match your own or that help you understand how other people are feeling.

And look out for the cat on every page. He has feelings too!

978-1-84780-281-1

"A terrific book – essential for schools and perfect for families" – Marilyn Brocklehurst, *Bookseller's Children's Choice*

Starred reviews from *Kirkus*, *Booklist*, *School Library Journal*

The Great Big Green Book

Your planet needs you!

Save water, save energy, recycle, ask questions – and help protect the forests, oceans, fresh water and wildlife on our planet.

With clear information about life on Earth and important conservation issues, accompanied by witty and wonderful illustrations, The Great Big Green Book is packed with ideas and inspiration for ways to keep our planet safe and beautiful for future generations of children.

978-1-84780-445-7

"An important and inspiring book" – *LoveReading*